The Courage To Carry On

Sermons For
Lent And Easter
During Cycle B

David H. Webb

CSS Publishing Company, Inc., Lima, Ohio

THE COURAGE TO CARRY ON

Copyright © 2009 by
CSS Publishing Company, Inc.
Lima, Ohio

All rights reserved. No part of this publication may be reproduced in any manner whatsoever without the prior permission of the publisher, except in the case of brief quotations embodied in critical articles and reviews. Inquiries should be addressed to: Permissions, CSS Publishing Company, Inc., 517 South Main Street, Lima, Ohio 45804.

Unless otherwise marked, scripture quotations are from the New Revised Standard Version of the Bible, copyright 1989 by the Division of Christian Education of the National Council of the Churches of Christ in the USA. Used by permission.

Scripture quotations marked (RSV) are from the Revised Standard Version of the Bible, copyrighted 1946, 1952 ©, 1971, 1973, by the Division of Christian Education of the National Council of the Churches of Christ in the USA. Used by permission.

Library of Congress Cataloging-in-Publication Data

Webb, David H., 1944-
  The courage to carry on : sermons for Lent and Easter during Cycle B / David H. Webb.
    p. cm.
  ISBN 0-7880-2601-1 (perfect bound : alk. paper)
  1. Easter—Sermons. 2. Lent—Sermons. 3. Common lectionary (1992). 4. Sermons, American—20th century. I. Title.
  BV55.W43 2009
  251'.6—dc22

2008027841

For more information about CSS Publishing Company resources, visit our website at www.csspub.com or email us at csr@csspub.com or call (800) 241-4056.

Cover design by Barbara Spencer
ISBN-13: 978-0-7880-2601-0
ISBN-10: 0-7880-2601-1   PRINTED IN USA

*To Karen
the joy of my life
in celebration of our
38th wedding anniversary*

Table Of Contents

Introduction   7
    by Wesley T. Runk

Ash Wednesday   9
    Our Journey Begins Again
    Joel 2:1-2, 12-17

Lent 1   13
    Relentless Grace
    Genesis 9:8-17

Lent 2   17
    An Incredible Blessing
    Genesis 17:1-7, 15-16

Lent 3   21
    A Precious Gift
    Exodus 20:1-17

Lent 4   25
    Lift High The Cross
    Numbers 21:4-9

Lent 5   29
    Planted In Our Hearts
    Jeremiah 31:31-34

Passion/Palm Sunday   33
    Salvation Is Coming
    Isaiah 50:4-9a

Maundy Thursday   37
    Slaves Set Free
    Exodus 12:1-4 (5-10) 11-14

Good Friday 39
    God's Incredible Gift
    Isaiah 52:13—53:12

Easter Day 41
    The Difference Easter Makes
    Acts 10:34-43

Easter 2 45
    The Church's DNA
    Acts 4:32-35

Easter 3 49
    At The Heart
    Acts 3:12-19

Easter 4 53
    Confident Faith
    Acts 4:5-12

Easter 5 57
    A Wonderful Conversion Story
    Acts 8:26-40

Easter 6 61
    Our Salvation In Being Loved
    Acts 10:44-48

The Ascension Of Our Lord 65
    Life's Greatest Tension: Despair vs. Hope
    Acts 1:1-11

Easter 7 69
    The Courage To Carry On
    Acts 1:15-17, 21-26

Introduction

The season of Lent is taken seriously by a multitude of Christians. It has formed habits of worship attendance different from any other time of the year. Lent embraces the liturgy offered by denominations, the sacraments as a holy moment of self-reflection, and encourages teaching and dialogue on a different level of faith. Many Christians file their devotions daily and even change their eating habits.

The humbled follower reflects on Lent as a time of personal examination of his/her discipleship. What began as a celebration of Christ's resurrection on the day after the sabbath is now preceded by the agony of Good Friday. It is also preceded by the institution of the Eucharist on Thursday, the plotting of God's enemies on Wednesday, the cleansing of the temple on Tuesday, and the welcoming parade on Sunday that revealed the misunderstanding of followers and antagonists on the coming kingdom on Palm Sunday.

One week is not enough to unburden us from the secular world. We have expanded our experience to six weeks of inspection. Each week has new meaning and drives us to Easter with quickening steps. It seems as though we just finished our celebration of Christmas when we are plunged into a time of mourning. The light is out there, Easter is coming, but we will not see the morning light and the empty tomb until we have examined the suffering of Jesus for our sakes.

What leads to Easter and concludes with the empty tomb is not a one-day event. Easter is the time we share with the resurrected Christ. It is not about looking over our shoulders and claiming that we believe in the only man who died and lived again. It is about the promise that we will be Easter people, also. We will also know the joy of not being restricted to a time or place. We can point to the promises that we will be one with Jesus and live the perfect life in heaven. Easter is a journey of time when we engage ourselves as part of the kingdom of God.

David Webb is a friend of only a few years past. We met in our retirement at Emmanuel Lutheran Church in Venice, Florida. I first met David when he was the interim between pastorates. He brings much to the table. As a retired general of the United States Air Force, he has the stature of someone who has received the approval of others. As a chaplain, he ministered to the needs of men and women in a time of war and peace. They knew him as a counselor and friend who could be counted on regardless of their fears and loneliness.

This book of sermons is not about him. This book is about what he does best and that is preach memorable sermons that make a difference to our week and our outlook on life. David Webb is someone who absorbs life moments and turns them into illustrations for living. His stories about life fit the point he is trying to make.

In the sermons for this Lenten and Easter season, you will discover a master storyteller, a scholar, and a preacher who will enable you to find new insights into the texts that you will preach.

I am very pleased to introduce you to Pastor David Webb, a friend and a leader of people committed to the ministry of Jesus Christ. Enjoy every moment of your experience.

— Wesley T. Runk
Retired pastor and publisher

Ash Wednesday
Joel 2:1-2, 12-17

Our Journey Begins Again

Once upon a time, tragedy struck a small church family where an eighteen-year-old boy took his own life. A suicide note was discovered that revealed a heartbreaking reality. The note said, in part, that the boy would rather die than to ask for help. He would rather die than to take a long, hard look at himself and expose his weaknesses to another person. He would rather die than to risk a change of heart and ask God for help. As extreme as that attitude seems, it's probably not uncommon. The miracle is that one could continue to live that way for a lifetime.[1]

Ash Wednesday reminds us that there is another way to live. There is another reality that appears to be rooted in weakness but in truth reveals a partnership that can sustain us through every chapter of life.

Tonight we begin another Lenten journey. We have an opportunity to begin a forty-day period of penance, renewal, and reflection about our faith and life in Jesus Christ.

The mood of our worship is somber and pensive. But the presence of Christ in our struggle is real and renewing. Hope abounds. Help is at hand.

Our scriptural text is from the prophet Joel.

Joel speaks of gloom, clouds, and thick darkness. "Yet even now, says the Lord, return to me with all your heart ... Return to the Lord, your God, for he is gracious and merciful, slow to anger, and abounding in steadfast love" (vv. 12-13b).

First and foremost, our Lenten journey is about good news.

Joel reminds us how the Lord is abounding in steadfast love. Good news! The forty days of Lent, the Passion of our Lord, the mystery of our redemption, and the gift of our baptism are all good news!

The presence of Christ in our lives and Christ's eagerness to save us, love us, and walk with us every day of our lives is good news!

The Lord's promise of forgiveness and the gift of life eternal are good news — extremely good news.

Secondly, our Lenten journey calls us to repentance. We are by nature selfish and self-serving.

Our pious gestures and self-indulgent appetites often deceive us and reveal something about us we dislike and struggle to deny.

There is a story of Savanarola, the great preacher of the fifteenth century, and an elderly woman who worshiped at the statue of the Virgin Mary that stood in his city's great cathedral. He saw her there day after day, on her knees paying homage to the Blessed Mary.

"Look how devoted she is to the Virgin Mother," Savanarola said to a fellow priest.

"Don't be deceived by what you see," the priest responded. "Many years ago, an artist was commissioned to create a statue for the cathedral. He looked for a woman to pose as a model for the sculpture. At last, he found one who seemed to be the perfect subject. Shortly after the statue was put in place, a woman came to visit it, knelt before it, to worship and adore the statue. One day, the woman lifted her veil. She was the woman who posed for the statue. She has come every day to kneel down before it ever since. What she comes to worship is herself!"[2]

Pride and self-centeredness can be terribly poisonous. Lent calls us to face the reality of our sin and repent. The ashes on our foreheads help us regain perspective.

Finally, our Lenten journey calls us to an entirely new way of living.

Often we interpret Lent to be very private. We understand the forty days to be a rigorous time of self-denial and self-discipline. Some of our childhood memories recall a time when we were confronted with the question, "What are you giving up for Lent?" There is nothing wrong with that, of course. But if our Lenten journey consists of only personal experiences, we miss the point! To be renewed by the love of God in Jesus Christ, to repent of our self-centered motives and condition, should always revitalize our faith and our way of living.

When the French philosopher and mathematician, Blaise Pascal, died in 1662, it was found that he had stitched a piece of parchment into his coat so that it would lie next to his heart. On the parchment paper was a cross surrounded by the rays of the rising sun. Under the cross he had written the year and day of his conversion to Christianity and the words, "I feel joy and peace."[3]

The patch was always close to his heart and always served as a reminder of the presence of the risen Christ in that heart.

Christ is alive in ours, too!

Our Lenten journey allows us once again to "return to the Lord"; to be aware of who lives in our heart; to embrace the love, mercy, and freedom that we have in Jesus Christ, our redeemer and Lord.

---

1. Bruce Larson, *The Presence* (Waco, Texas: Word Books, 1988), p. 50.

2. *Parish Publications, Inc.* (Madison Heights, Michigan: Parish Publications, 1992), p. 3.

3. www.catholic.org/encyclopedia/view.php?id=9011.

Lent I
Genesis 9:8-17

Relentless Grace

The story of old Noah and his ark has been told to children and adults for centuries. It has intrigued us, taught us, and even amused us. Bill Cosby's depiction of the dialogue between Noah and God is classic! So are other cartoons and renditions.

The Lord said to Noah, "Where is the ark I commanded you to build?" And Noah said, "Verily, I had three carpenters off sick and the gopherwood supplier hast let me down, even though gopherwood hath been on order for nigh on twelve months." And God said to Noah, "I want the ark finished before seven days and seven nights," and Noah said, "It will be so." And it was not so. The Lord said to Noah, "What seems to be the trouble this time?" And Noah said, "My subcontractor hath gone bankrupt, the pitch for the outside hath not arrived, the glazer departeth on holiday, yea though I offered him double time. Lord, I am undone." The Lord grew angry and said, "What about the animals? Two of every sort I ordered. Where are the giraffes?" And Noah said, "They have been delivered to the wrong address but should arrive on Friday." On and on the story goes, one mishap after another.[1]

The Noah's ark story is a wonderful story. On the one hand, it relates humankind's relentless determination to resist and even abuse its relationship with God. On the other hand, the story reveals a very significant truth about God's persistent love and eagerness to ensure a faithful relationship with all his children.

It has been reported over and again that God's people are stiff-necked, impatient, sinful, unfaithful, disobedient, and selfish. Such was surely the case in our story. God is displeased and heartbroken because of it. Certainly it occurs again and again throughout history.

Have you ever been to the Holocaust Museum in Washington DC? It is a gray, graphic memorial to the horrors of the World War II death camps. It will take your breath away. The walls and corridors are filled with reminders of man's inhumanity to man. As one visits places like that, it is easy to understand how at some point in history God might have said, "I can't take it anymore. Enough is enough. I shall destroy this creation that has become so evil."

Such was the case in our story of Noah, but it never happened again. In fact, God's promise to Noah was so strong that God promised that the flood would never be repeated.

God said, "This is the sign of the covenant which I make between me and you and every living creature ... for all future generations. I set my bow in the cloud, and it shall be a sign of the covenant between me and the earth" (vv. 12-13).

The promise as revealed in the rainbow is yet another example of how God is determined to save us. The salvation history of God throughout scripture tells one story after another of God's relentless grace. Covenant after covenant, God takes initiative. Forgiveness and renewal are offered. New beginnings are negotiated. God never gives up.

The cycle continues until finally God sends his only Son to establish an everlasting covenant ... a covenant that is permanent!

Jesus Christ is our ark —☐our salvation.

The cross of Christ, like the rainbow, is our sign of hope and promise.

We will never get it right by ourselves. But through Christ our Lord we have assurance, the baptismal promise of redemption and the everlasting presence of one who will always love us and set us free.

God's grace is a powerful reality in our lives! It's a mystery, but as it unfolds we discover a wonderful relief from the notion that we must do something to save ourselves.

Robert Capon expresses it so beautifully.

The salt mine is closed. You are dead to the law by the body of Christ. This means that it is not only you who *are dead and beyond the orbit of blame; but God, too. God, himself, the supreme lawgiver, blamefixer, and guiltspreader, has died to the whole sorry business in the death of Jesus. There is, therefore, no condemnation. It does not matter what the universe thinks. It does not matter what other people think. It does not matter what you think. It does not even matter what God thinks because God has said that he was not going to think about it anymore. All he thinks now is Jesus, Jesus, Jesus; and Jesus is now all your life. You are therefore free.*²

We are truly free to live a new life in Jesus Christ our Lord! That's the gospel to the fullest!

Sometimes it takes a lifetime to surrender and embrace this overwhelming gift but as we do life is never the same.

A letter from Nadine Star, an 85-year-old woman in Kentucky, puts the insight of freedom in vivid terms. If she could live her life over again, she says, she would.

*Dare to make more mistakes next time. I'd relax. I would limber up. I would be sillier than I have been this trip. I would take fewer things seriously. I would take more chances. I'd climb more mountains and swim more rivers. I'd eat more ice cream. I would perhaps have more actual troubles but I'd have fewer imaginary ones. You see, I'm one of those people who lives sensibly and sanely hour after hour, day after day. Oh, I've had my moments, and if I had it to do over again, I'd have more of them. I've been one of those persons who never goes anywhere without a thermometer, a hot water bottle, a raincoat, and a parachute. I would travel lighter next time ... If I had my life to live over, I'd start barefoot earlier in the spring and stay that way later in the fall. I'd go to more dances; I'd ride more merry-go-rounds; I'd pick more daisies.*³

The new life in Christ may offer such perspective, as Nadine Star would have it. But it goes even further, doesn't it? God has fixed everything in Jesus Christ. We have life now and forever in his name.

---

1. Bruce Larson, *My Creator, My Friend* (Waco, Texas: Word Books, 1986), pp. 42-43.

2. Robert F. Capon, *Between Noon and Three: A Parable of Romance, Law, and the Outrage of Grace* (New York: Harper and Row, 1982), p. 118.

3. William Lenters, *The Freedom We Crave* (Grand Rapids, Michigan: William B. Eerdmans Publishing Company, 1985), p. 123.

Lent 2
Genesis 17:1-7, 15-16

An Incredible Blessing

When I was in the second grade, I won a Bible storybook by selling magazines. It was illustrated with colored pictures unlike the King James Bible from which my mother read our nightly bedtime stories. It was a significant improvement. I was very pleased.

Bible bedtime stories are very formative. Mostly they teach us about God, his love, mercy, expectations, and blessing. They also teach us how to live. They even plant seeds.

Our Bible story today is very familiar. It is the story of Abraham and Sarah depicting how they were chosen by God to be blessed in order that they might be a blessing. "Behold, my covenant is with you, and you shall be the father (and mother) of a multitude of nations ... I will make you exceedingly fruitful ... and give you the land of Canaan."

Quite a blessing, isn't it? Life would never be the same for them. They soon left home on a mission trip that eventually changed them and the world.

In our Judeo-Christian tradition, Abraham and Sarah have become the classic examples of faith. They recognized the voice of God. They understood the voice of God. They trusted in God's purpose for their lives and followed in faith and obedience.

As we reflect over these faithful servants of the Lord, we recognize the big challenges for our own lives. Where am I going with my life? How has God's choices and blessings for me shaped my journey so far? What is it that God wants me to do in the future? Not always as easy as it was for Abraham and Sarah.

Soren Kierkegaard once remarked, "What I really lack is to be clear in my mind what I am to do, not what I am to know ... The thing is to understand myself, to see what God really wishes me to do ... to find the idea for which I can live and die."

How can we do that?

I suppose one approach is to develop a personal mission statement. God can certainly speak to us as we discern through a more structured means.

Stephen Covey, author of *The Seven Habits of Highly Effective People*, suggests that as we develop a personal mission statement, we should focus on our values and principles that are central to our lives. We should add as a primary principle, faith and focus on what God has in mind.

Peter Drucker suggests that we focus on two very important questions in helping us discover the unique role God wants us to explore. The questions are:

1. What have you already achieved? (competence)
2. What do you care deeply about? (passion)

The goal is to find something, through prayer, that fits something you're good at and something that excites you.

An excellent book to help discover one's life mission is titled, *What Color is Your Parachute?* by Dick Bolles. An ordained Episcopal priest, Bolles has a helpful chapter in his book titled, "How to Find Your Mission in Life."[1]

The important aspect of this little exercise, as with any discernment process about our purpose and future, is to struggle in both prayer and petition to hear God's voice and sense God's leading. God has a purpose for all of us, and when it happens, satisfaction and joy often occur.

But remember that God always takes the initiative and he usually approaches busy people. Sometimes we think that if we take a week off and go to the monastery, God might break through to us and we might catch a new vision. Such belief, however, is not biblically sound. God's call to Moses came when he was busy with his sheep at Horeb. Gideon was busy threshing wheat. Saul was busy searching for his father's lost animals. Elisha was busy plowing. David was busy caring for his father's flock. Amos was busy picking figs. James and John were mending nets. Lydia was busy marketing and selling fabrics. Peter and Andrew were fishing. Matthew was collecting taxes. Mary and Elizabeth were busy with their homemaking. On and on God issues a call in a specific way for a unique task. He hasn't changed. When we are in a position to listen carefully and move out with our God-given abilities trusting obediently, great things can happen.

Dag Hammarskjöld once said, "I don't know who — or, what — put the question — I don't know when it was put. I don't even remember answering. But at some moment I did answer yes to someone — or — something — and from that hour I was certain that existence is meaningful and that, therefore my life, in self-surrender, had a purpose."

Albert Schweitzer was a brilliant theologian. He held PhDs in several fields, including theology, music, medicine, and philosophy. He even wrote a book titled *A Quest for the Historical Jesus*. In the midst of all this success, Schweitzer heard an irresistible call from God to be a medical missionary in a small rural village in Africa. The rest is history. He spent the rest of his life there and the hospital continues to thrive.

A small-town country lawyer from Georgia sensed a call from God to do something about housing for the world's poor. Did you know that half of the people in the world either have no place to live or dwell in miserable substandard housing? Millard Fuller said, "We can change that." In a little over twenty years, Habitat for Humanity has made a significant dent by this powerful ministry. Homes have been built in scores of overseas communities and practically every state in this nation. We need to wonder whom will God call next to make a difference in some small way in our broken world.

Are you listening? Would you like to be more fulfilled in your life and responsive to your faith? I think God has a plan for all of us. Perhaps not as grandiose as was the case with Abraham, David, Schweitzer, and Fuller but significant, purposeful, and rewarding.

George Bernard Shaw once said, "Life is no brief candle to me. It's a sort of splendid torch which I've got hold of for the moment, and I want to make it burn as brightly as possible before handing it over to future generations."

---

1. Dick Bolles, *What Color is Your Parachute?* (Berkeley, California: Ten Speed Press, 2003 [revised]).

Lent 3
Exodus 20:1-17

A Precious Gift

Some time ago, *National Geographic* printed a feature article on the Appalachian Trail. This national treasure is a hiking trail 2,175 miles long that goes from Spring Mountain, Georgia, basically along the Blue Ridge and Appalachian Mountains all the way to Mount Katahdin, Maine.

The opening story was about a young man who began his journey in late April at the base of Springer Mountain. His objectives were twofold:

1. To successfully complete his awesome wilderness journey by fall.
2. "To find himself."

He arrived at the top of Mount Katahdin five months later, only to discover that after all the reflection and solitude, all the spent energy, he had *not* found himself. Perplexed and mentally and emotionally exhausted, he turned around and hiked all the way back to Georgia, arriving the following spring. And guess what? He still had *not* found himself. True story.

In our text for today the people of Israel were hiking in the wilderness. They were on a twofold mission:

1. To reach the promised land.
2. To grow in faith and identity as God's chosen people.

As we contemplate the Exodus story and the situation in which the people of Israel found themselves, it seems appropriate to ask why God gave them the Ten Commandments. What was the big deal?

Scholars tell us there are two primary reasons.

One reason centered on the challenge of survival and living together as a people. They had been in the wilderness for several years. There had been tensions, rebellions, disobedience, altercations, and times of disillusionment! They became physically, mentally, and emotionally weary. It was a good time to hear from God, so God sent them a gift — The Ten Commandments. First and foremost, they begin with good news, "I am the Lord your God, who brought you out of the land of Egypt, out of the house of slavery" (v. 2). God's love and renewal of promise always seems to come first. The children of Israel and God's people throughout the ages always find their way as they remember the promises and allow God to renew their faith.

Secondly, the Ten Commandments became a catechism in the wilderness that helped the people of Israel continue to be faithful to God and respectful of one another. Both were essential for their survival.

It's the same for us along our journey. Sometimes it's tough. The distractions are abundant. The temptations are relentless and very seductive. However, we know that obedience to good directions and following Jesus is a great way to live.

Fred Craddock once told a cute story about sitting in church one hot summer night with the windows open. He was listening to the preacher drone away when a man came by the church building and stopped by the window and said, "Psst, psst." Fred responded, "What is it? I'm listening to the sermon." The man responded, "Come with me. I know where there is a pearl of great price that's more valuable than all other pearls in the world. In fact, where I am going, there is treasure buried in a field and even bums are invited to sit at the king's table. Come, go with me."

Fred argued with the man a bit, listened to the rest of the sermon, then spoke with the preacher after the service. He told the preacher how he was disturbed and hoped it didn't upset him during his sermon. The preacher asked Fred who the man was and if he was getting anybody to join him. And Fred said, "Well, none of our crowd went, but I noticed he had about twelve with him."[1]

The twelve disciples were certainly familiar with the joys and challenges of following Jesus. They understood the expectations. They were beginning to understand what it meant to be a team. Above all, they understood the strength and grace that held it all together through Jesus Christ, our Lord.

The Ten Commandments are a precious gift, and the gospel of Jesus Christ is even greater.

Both are about God who loves the people he created.

Both are about God who promises to be faithful in love to each of us, all sealed in the blood of our Lord.

Both are about relationships we share as God's people.

And it is all a *gift*!

As we reflect on God's gifts to us, there should be a certain freedom that occurs in our hearts. But occasionally there arises a tension in this freedom — this sense of security in God's promises on the one hand and a sense of accountability to God on the other. Some see the Ten Commandments as a means of accountability and a reminder that God requires perfection. Such perception can produce fear, which may not be what God fully desires. In fact, it just might be that fear is the one thing that God desires most to abolish because it can be so destructive.

Once upon a time, a very devout Christian confessed that he was often haunted by a terrible dream. He dreamed that while traveling in a particular city he ran into an old high school classmate. In the bad dream, the person would ask, "Henri, Henri, haven't seen you in years. What have you done with your life?" The question always felt like judgment. He had done some remarkable things in his life, but there had been some struggles and misfortunes. So when the old schoolmate in the dream would ask, "What have you done with your life?" Henri didn't know what to say, how to account for his life. Then one night he had another dream. He dreamed that he was waiting outside the throne room of God, waiting to stand before the almighty, shivering with fear. He just knew that God would be surrounded with fire and smoke and would speak with a deep voice saying, "Henri, Henri, what have you done with your life?" Then, in the dream, when the door to God's throne room opened, the room was filled with light. From the room he could hear God speaking to him in a gentle voice saying, "Henri, Henri, it's good to see you. I hear you had a rough trip ... but I'd love to see your slides."[2]

As we reflect over the gifts, let's remember the goodness and the grace of God, most of all! His love and mercy endures forever.

---

1. Fred Craddock, *Craddock Stories* (St. Louis, Missouri: Chalice Press, 2001), p. 36.

2. www.day1.net/index.php5?view=transcripts&tid=34.

Lent 4
Numbers 21:4-9

Lift High The Cross

In our story today, the children of Israel are simply tired and worn out. Their wilderness journey to the promised land had overwhelmed them. They were exhausted and put out with Moses and God. They were impatient and probably afraid. Finally, there was an eruption: "Why have you brought us up out of Egypt to die in this wilderness? For there is no food and no water, and we detest this miserable food" (v. 5).

In their weakness, they lost composure, mistrusted their leaders, and fell back into the *if only* position. *If only* we had stayed in Egypt. *If only* we had a different leader. *If only* God could be trusted.

Most likely, the people of Israel were terribly afraid.

Henri Nouwen has said that "the agenda of the world — the issues and items that fill newspapers and newscasts — is an agenda of fear."[1] It is amazing, even frightening, how that agenda can so easily become our agenda especially when we are tired and exhausted. Consider all the *if* questions that arise when we are anxious and afraid: What if I lose my job? What will happen if I get sick or an accident happens? What if I can't pay all the bills? What if my marriage fails? How can I rear my children in a culture that is so violent and immoral? On and on the anxious, fearful questions confront us. It is not difficult to understand how the Israelites must have felt. It's tough to keep the perspective when we are drained, depleted, and near collapse.

At that juncture, I suppose God felt like he had to do something to divert their doldrums, to snap them out of it. So he sent the serpent that eventually evolved into a bronze serpent on a pole to serve as a reminder of his promises and presence. God got their attention. Trust and purpose were restored.

It works the same for us sometimes. We need to be reminded of a greater reality, shocked sometimes into this awareness.

In his beautiful little book, *My Creator, My Friend*, Bruce Larson invites the reader to walk with him into the home of a new mother.

She asks you to come in while she bathes the baby. The kitchen looks like a disaster area. The baby is in the bassinet. There's water all over the floor. There is cereal everywhere, even up the wall. The sink is full of eggshells and burnt toast and dirty dishes. In the midst of this mess, she catches you looking at the blue ribbon over the sink on which hangs a Phi Beta Kappa key. "Ah, you noticed," she says. "I hung it there to remind myself that if I was smart enough to get that, I'm smart enough to get myself out of this present mess."[2]

We may not be a Phi Beta Kappa, but God has other signs and reminders of the gospel he has in store for all his children.

God is able to deal with the mess we are in and all the *if onlys* that erupt from our anxious hearts. God is able. God is faithful. God is determined to save us all.

The apostle Paul captures the release that can be ours in his letter to the Romans: "Who shall separate us from the love of Christ? Shall tribulation, or distress, or persecution, or famine, or nakedness, or peril, or sword? ... No, in all these things we are more than conquerors through him who loved us. For I am sure that neither death, nor life, nor angels, nor powers, nor height, nor depth, nor anything else in all creation, will be able to separate us from the love of God in Christ Jesus our Lord" (Romans 8:35b, 37-39 RSV).

The cross of Christ is our standard, our reminder of God's redemption in Jesus Christ. A bronze cross instead of bronze serpent leads our procession of honor and thanksgiving. As we follow and take it all in, we have our hope restored and our faith renewed. We can say with Paul, "We know that in everything God works for good with those who love him and who are called according to his purpose" (Romans 8:28 RSV).

Wonderful news!

Some time ago, I read about a man who was involved in an accident on the freeway. His car was sideswiped by a sports car driven by an attractive young woman. Neither party was hurt, but the other driver was distraught. "This is a brand new car. My husband just bought it for me. He'll be heartbroken." Eventually, the police came and, in the process of exchanging registration and insurance papers, a note fell out of the glove compartment of the young woman's car. It was written by her husband and this was the message: "Darling, if you ever need to use these papers, remember that it's you I love and not the car."

What foresight. What a splendid way to displace anguish and fear with love.

This is where God wants us to live: loved, forgiven, empowered, refreshed, and redeemed through the cross of Christ.

John writes in his first letter: "Perfect love casts out fear!" (1 John 4:18). We have that love in Christ Jesus our Lord.

Nouwen states that we often become so accustomed to living in fear that we become deaf to the voice that says: "Do not be afraid." This reassuring voice repeats itself over and over again. "Do not be afraid. Have no fear, little flock."

Lift high the cross!

---

1. Henri Nouwen, *Lifesigns* (New York: Doubleday and Co., 1986), pp. 16-17.

2. Bruce Larson, *My Creator, My Friend* (Waco, Texas: Word Books, 1986), p. 157.

Lent 5
Jeremiah 31:31-34

Planted In Our Hearts

Once upon a time, at a pastor and teacher's conference the group leader asked everyone present to identify the most influential person, other than parents, in the spiritual formation of their lives. It was difficult for some to choose. Dr. Fred Craddock was participating in the exercise. When it came his turn to share, he stood up and said, "Her name was Miss Emma Sloan." Craddock went on to describe Miss Emma Sloan as an elderly single woman. "She taught me in the primary department," related Craddock. "And since there was nobody to teach us as juniors, she went right on with us, and taught us for years. She gave me a Bible. She wrote in the front: 'May this be a light to your feet, a lamp for your path. Emma Sloan.' She taught us to memorize the Bible; she never tried to interpret it. I don't remember her ever explaining anything. She just said, 'Just put it in your heart. Just put it in your heart.' "[1]

Dr. Craddock concluded by describing how Miss Emma's influence of memorizing Bible verses, planted in his heart, has sustained his life over and over again. Some of us have similar experiences. There is something about having the good news of God planted in our hearts that makes a difference.

As we approach the end of our season of penance and preparation, Jeremiah anticipates a primary thrust of the Easter experience, in that God will transform human hearts. Jeremiah's vision of this new covenant follows the dreadful time of suffering in the Babylonian exile. Similar to that time of crisis and suffering, during the transition time between passion and resurrection, a vision of hope and good news is announced. Judgment is not the final word. A new covenant is coming.

"The days are surely coming, says the Lord, when I will make a new covenant ..." (v. 31). It will not be like the old covenant ...

"This covenant ... will put my law within them, and I will write it on their hearts; and I will be their God and they shall be my people" (v. 33).

The language is very intimate, isn't it? "I will write the new covenant in their hearts; and I will be their God and they shall be my people."

Miss Emma Sloan knew exactly what she was doing as she encouraged her students to memorize selected scripture verses by heart. It was a quickening of something already there; a reinforcement of promises planted long ago.

We are God's people. God is faithfully connected and active in our lives. His loving presence resides in our hearts. We, in turn, come to life in spirit and in purpose as we respond to this intimate loving relationship.

Saint John of the Cross of the sixteenth century coined the phrase, "the dark night of the soul." His awareness suggests dark times in anyone's life when there is fear, depression, and despair. Perhaps this was the case during the time of the Babylonian exile and perhaps especially during our time.

But with the covenants, promises, and activity of God especially in Jesus Christ our Lord, we can be renewed and reshaped from the inside out.

Sometimes it comes as a slow but steady discovery that the steadfast love of God never fails. This love of God in Christ seems to be most evident when we are aware of the merciful presence of Christ in our lives. It seems to be incarnational, planted in our hearts. Quite often, God appears to be most real to people who are struggling with difficulties that seem too much for them. In the midst of such turbulence and discouragement, they often discover that God has not abandoned them.

This spiritual sensitivity and awareness can save us from cynicism and despair by the quiet realization that our Savior and Lord will never forsake us.

William Hinson, in an inspiring book titled, *Reshaping the Inner You*, speaks of being transformed by the power of God's love in our hearts. Hinson indicates that too many of us have forgotten that life is lived from the *inside*.

"On our way to achieving the outward signs of success, we've forgotten or neglected the spirit. We are like the prodigal son, who fed one part of his being and starved another. That's why we wind up in the pigpen of life. We are not just a body; we are spirit as well. By choosing to take God's path, no matter what your age or station in life, you can begin to live again from the inside."[2]

Susan was a beautiful woman. She enjoyed sports of all kinds, especially water sports. Since her father owned a boat company, Susan spent many afternoons on the lake skiing behind one of the fastest and finest ski boats on the water. But tragedy was lurking.

One day Susan was out riding in a car with her brother, John. She was happy and full of life. In fact, it was her sixteenth birthday. Before she knew what happened, there was a scream of brakes and a clash of metal. Immediately she was knocked unconscious.

When Susan awoke, in a daze of pain, bright lights filled her room. The intravenous bottle, people all around her dressed in white, and the smell of antiseptic suggested to her that she was in a hospital emergency room. She tried to shift. Her legs would not move. Weak with pain, she shut her eyes.

As consciousness grew, she became more aware of voices and a conversation just outside her room. To her shock and horror she heard someone telling her father, "Your daughter's legs are paralyzed." There was a long silence broken by deep crying by her father.

Some moments later, her father, other family members, and the doctor gathered around Susan's bed to tell her the truth. Her father, so pale and downcast, took Susan's hand and said, "Honey, you will never walk again."

In those few devastating moments before they came into the room, Susan had prayed. A remarkable calm had interceded. Because she had experienced merciful strength from God before, somehow she was able to blurt out, "I can still use my hands."

From that moment forward, Susan began an upward journey. There were doubts, despair, cries of anguish mixed with hope, prayers, and trust in the good Lord's mercy and healing. Every morning she had her devotions. And every morning she determined to fix her eyes on the things other than her personal tragedy. With a deep awareness of Christ in her heart and fully confident in the Lord's mercy, Susan persevered. She returned to school and completed an accounting degree at Rice University. Eventually, she married and had two children. Her life has become an inspiration, a joy, and a comfort to those who know her.[3]

Susan's story is a wonderful story. It reminds us how joy, hope, perspective, endurance, and faith can be ours as well, under any circumstances, because we have the gifts of God in our hearts. We have an inward capacity to see life and love life with courage and insight because this new covenant has become a reality we can count on.

---

1. Fred Craddock, *Craddock Stories* (St. Louis, Missouri: Chalice Press, 2001), pp. 33-34.

2. William Hinson, *Reshaping the Inner You* (San Francisco: Harper and Row, 1988), p. 16.

3. *Ibid*, pp. 21-22.

Passion/Palm Sunday
Isaiah 50:4-9a

Salvation Is Coming

There is something about this day that stirs us to the very depths of our being.

Perhaps it is the drama of a most unusual parade with the pathos of a lowly figure riding fearlessly into the jaws of death.

Perhaps it's the festive music and green palm branches that evoke the memory of a day in our own lives when we said yes to Christ —□confessing in our confirmation vows that Jesus Christ is Lord and redeemer, pledging to serve him and to love him forever.

Perhaps it's simply an exciting moment of the Lenten drama that we know will burst forth in joy and celebration only one week from now.

The excitement was incredible on the first Palm Sunday. The scripture says the whole city was stirred. Can we see why? For one thing, the city was in a state of hypertension at that particular time, both religiously and politically. The pious were swelling with religious enthusiasm as the pilgrims poured into the city to keep the great national festival of the Passover. The nationals were preparing for a revolution, which they thought for sure would happen. The collaborators, like Herod, were playing the game with Rome as well as they could, trying to keep one foot in each world. The religious leaders were trying their best to protect the beloved establishment, to save it from destruction. Caiaphas was chief among them.

Into that tense situation, with friction so great that you can almost feel it, went Jesus in a way not likely to calm things down.

He was a young man in the prime of life riding on a beast of burden, reminding every good Jew what the prophets had said, "Lo, your king comes to you; triumphant and victorious is he, humble and riding on a donkey" (Zechariah 9:9).

The prophet Isaiah uses language that mirrors the temperament and determination of our procession: "The Lord God helps me; therefore I have not been disgraced; therefore I have set my face like flint, and I know that I shall not be put to shame; he who vindicates me is near" (Isaiah 50:7-8).

This is the third of the servant songs set at the very end of the Babylonian exile. The Lord is about to do a new thing. Like the old exodus, the Lord is about to set his people free. Salvation is at hand.

Our parade contains a similar drama of anticipation. The Lord is about to do something sensational. Salvation is on its way.

One of the most interesting aspects of all the drama was the fact that what the people saw and expected was far different from whom Jesus really was and what he truly represented. They were looking for a Messiah who would put them back in power. His idea of a Messiah was a person who would put them into service, put them to use. They were thinking of a Messiah who would restore the national grandeur of the nation. He was thinking of a Messiah who would take a life of unselfish suffering and through it, transform and inspire a people to live differently. They didn't understand. Even his closest friends were not exceptionally perceptive. They, too, missed the point.

Peter came close once, when Jesus asked the question, "Who do you say that I am?" Peter responded, "You are the Messiah" (Mark 8:27-29). But then, when Jesus began to speak about the Messiah in terms of suffering, Peter rebuked him. He missed the point.

Let's turn from Jerusalem to where we live for a moment, specifically to all who have gathered to watch the parade and hear the Passion scriptures read again.

Who is he? What is this pageantry, which leads to incredible suffering all about?

We think we know. We say that he is Jesus Christ, God's Son, our Lord. We profess that he is the Savior of the world, and that he suffered and died for our sins.

We know infinitely more about him than the first Palm Sunday crowd. We certainly ought to, for we have had a long time to think about him. Yet, his life, his death, the entire drama is just too much for us to fully comprehend.

Historically we've made the day a mini-Easter of sorts, waving our palm branches primarily for the wrong reasons, avoiding the thought of what's really happening and what it means.

Peter's way seems to be the better way, doesn't it? Recognizing Jesus as the Messiah of power and glory in a kingly rule. That's what we need in this broken, mixed-up world.

But Peter was wrong and so are we. God knows best. His way is a better way: A way of redemption, love, and mercy.

This kingdom is different. It is not a kingdom of jihad or force or power or even self-serving interests and agendas but of love, mercy, and service.

A number of years ago, in a Minneapolis courtroom, sat a rebellious young man who had disgraced himself and his family. The young man had looked for an excuse for his predicament, not unusual to see such an intense self-serving appetite. He pointed his finger at his father, blaming him for insensitivity by saying, "He was just too busy to give me a second thought." The truth was that the son had misread his father for his own selfish reasons.

As the trial progressed, the son was made aware that his father had mortgaged his home to pay the legal fees, pleaded for a second chance before the district attorney for his boy, and sat by him throughout the exhausting proceedings. When a favorable verdict was returned, the boy broke down in uncontrollable sobs — clinging to his father. After he got a hold of himself, he said, "God, how I made you suffer. I never knew how much you loved me."[1]

If Christ had accepted the crown on Palm Sunday, would we have known how much God loves us? It is not a crown of kingly glory that you see upon that altar. It is the cross of God's caring and incredible love.

---

1. Robert Borgwardt, "A Most Unusual Parade," sermon preached on Palm Sunday, 1986, Madison, Wisconsin.

Maundy Thursday
Exodus 12:1-4 (5-10) 11-14

Slaves Set Free

It is believed that the Passover was first celebrated on the very night that Israel was set free from Egypt. Since that time, including the time of Jesus, the people of Israel have remembered that they were slaves set free by God.

Rescued and redeemed, the connections are solidified as Jesus lifts the cup and blesses the bread. "Take and eat. Drink from this cup."

Tonight the setting is the Garden of Gethsemane and the upper room. Jesus is celebrating the Passover with his disciples. The event would become known as the Last Supper thereafter. Let's crack open the door for a moment and peek inside.

Let's consider Jesus in relationship to those who were with him.

Picture them — Peter, Judas, Thomas, and the sons of Zebedee: James and John.

Some sat smugly folding their hands, pondering positions of influence in the new kingdom. Others sat with clenched fists, lest they reveal any sign of weakness. One, at least, was anticipating a devious plot.

Jesus was surely aware of all the motives and distractions. But scripture reminds us how he took a basin, a cup, and a loaf of bread. In this humble yet powerful way, Jesus is reinforcing what he taught them all along: love, service, compassion, sacrifice, discipline, peace of heart and soul, and a presence that would sustain them. We gather for the same perspective, the same peace, and the same presence.

We, too, have gathered with all our needs and insecurities on this sacred day to watch and witness, to receive the blessing of his real presence, and to be transformed and refocused.

The intimacy and the witness of the passion returns our hearts to where they ought to be. We know that. That's why we are here.

I read somewhere of a tape recording that is used in maternity wards to stop the crying of certain babies. When one infant after the other begins to howl, within moments they all are quiet. What do you imagine? Is it music? Is it a certain theme that is played? No! It is a recording of the mother's heartbeat as heard by the fetus within the womb before it was born. Apparently the infant's cry of discomfort and fear is stilled by the sense of security invoked by the sound of a mother's heartbeat.

We gather to receive this gift of our Lord's real presence again. It is an intimate affair. There is a spiritual linkage that has a way of reducing the fear and anxiety in our lives in addition to reconnecting us with a strength of renewal and purpose this world can never give.

Good Friday
Isaiah 52:13—53:12

God's Incredible Gift

The servant song in our Old Testament lesson from Isaiah has been the traditional Old Testament reading for Good Friday for a long time. No other text describes the Messiah as a suffering servant of God more clearly.

God presents the servant as his chosen one and suggests that he intends to exalt him through a mission of suffering for a greater purpose.

As we reflect on this special portion of scripture and the events of this holy day, may we always remember first and foremost that the suffering servant suffers and dies for others. The death, the agony, the abuse is vicarious. "He was crushed for our iniquities ... and by his bruises we are healed" (Isaiah 53:5).

Secondly, the drama of the suffering servant is depicted to bring about an awareness of the love of God and a conversion in all that witness it.

Like all the witnesses through the years, we gather to observe the agony and death and to realize once again that the suffering and death is for us. We are guilty. He is innocent. God is at work to redeem us in spite of our sin. In a real sense, the servant song becomes our confession.

There is a tremendous depth of feeling and drama in every Good Friday worship. We may not understand it all but we most always are moved to confession by God's incredible gift in Jesus our Lord.

The novelist, Frederick Buechner, once wondered what would happen if God, instead of depending upon our faith, decided to give us proof. What if God decided to clear up all this religion business and give us something scientific, something tangible, that would be beyond the shadow of a doubt? "Suppose," Buechner imagined, "that God were to take the great, dim river of the Milky Way — stars flowing across the night sky — and were to brighten it up a little and then rearrange it so that all of a sudden one night the world would step outside and look up at the heavens and see not the usual haphazard scattering of stars, but written out in letters light years tall the sentence: *I really exist.*"[1]

Well, most likely the reaction would be earth-shattering. Churches would grow like crazy. Crime would stop. Wars would cease. The frenzied anxious tenor of the world would settle down. This would go on for sometime until we took the clear proclamation, "I really exist," for granted. We might say, "So what?" What difference does it make?

Buechner goes on to say that we are not so interested in scientific proof that God really exists as we are in a personal awareness of God's presence and love for us as individuals. Then it hits home. Our faith is renewed and made much stronger.[2]

There may be a lot of questions about this day but at the center is God, knee deep in our sin, suffering, agonizing, and dying to redeem us all. The event is huge in the scope of what God intends for the world. It is very personal, as this Christ who dies for each of us, loves us beyond all comprehension.

---

1. http://www.day1.net/inex.php5?view=transcripts&tid=29.

2. *Ibid.*

Easter Day
Acts 10:34-43

The Difference Easter Makes

Once upon a time, a few years ago, a little boy came up to his pastor during Holy Week and said, "Say, pastor, anything special happening on Easter?" The pastor smiled at his innocent question and stooped to respond: "Matthew, you'll be surprised. Just wait and see. You won't believe it!"

The early risers on that first Easter morning were certainly surprised! They discovered something that was much more than *special*. It was life changing.

For twenty centuries, we Christians have celebrated this holy day. Hoards of people pack churches throughout the world to worship and remember an event that much of the world finds unimpressive and irrelevant. But we continue to find relevance and profound hope for our day-to-day living. An empty tomb, a few startled women, an angel of promise, and the renewed faith of followers and friends have passed along tremendous meaning for us. *Christ is risen! He is alive and always will be forevermore!*

The power of Christ's resurrection makes a big difference in our understanding of life and the way we live it.

In the first place, *we have hope*. Easter fills us with hope and lots of it!

Someone once wrote, "People can live forty days without food, about three days without water, about eight minutes without air, but only a second without hope."

Allowing for a slight exaggeration, the point is well taken. Hope is critical for human life.

Easter living is hope-filled living. Because of Christ's resurrection, we believe that there will always be a way through, a way out, a way over any obstacle, any pain, any misfortune, or any death.

Sinclair Lewis once wrote, "Life is a silly motion picture that doesn't make any difference which way you run it, backwards or forwards." In every age, there seems to be this chorus of ambivalence, unbelief, and even despair. Hope becomes critical during those times.

In the early church, people were extremely eager to hear the good news. Our first lesson story today tells of Peter's invitation to speak at the home of Cornelius and his family. Lots of folks were invited to be present. A nice crowd had gathered to hear an eyewitness to all that had taken place in Jerusalem. Peter preaches a dramatic sermon on the events and the power of Jesus Christ. The sermon was so candid and powerful that one could sense that something was happening to Peter as he preached.

Scholars tell us that through this experience at Cornelius' house Peter's world was suddenly changed to understand that Jesus Christ was Lord of all. The gospel was available to transform any life, any situation, any struggle with hopelessness.

There is no greater message to the world than Christ is risen in power. Because he lives we shall live, also. Hope abounds and we are no longer afraid and bewildered.

Secondly, because of Easter we have the presence of Christ with us forever.

The disciples thought it was over, nowhere to go, scared, perplexed, and terribly distraught.

But not for long! Their experience with him had only begun.

Christ's risen presence with us is an everlasting reality that will always make a big difference.

That brilliant, sophisticated Englishman with the funny name of Malcolm Muggeridge, who came to faith in Christ in mid-life, knows the difference Easter makes. In many ways, he was a typical product of our culture, the highly intellectualized society of the Western world. He began his career as a university lecturer, moved into journalism, and became the editor of *Punch* magazine. He was also a television personality and the director of Edinburgh University. But gradually Muggeridge began to find that the fruits of success were not enough. Something was missing. In spite of having so much, his heart was empty. He wrote in his autobiography,

Chronicles of Wasted Time, "Somehow, I missed you, God. You called me, and I didn't answer all those empty years."

The breakthrough came while he was filming *BC*, the story of Jesus, on location in Israel. One day, he and a friend walked the six miles between Jerusalem and Emmaus. It was along that same road that the presence of Jesus joined two men so long ago. It happened again. Two thousand years later for Muggeridge and his friend, there was a powerful revelation. Here are his words: "As my friend and I walked, like Cleopas and his friend we recalled, as they did, the events of the crucifixion of Jesus in light of our different, and yet similar world. Was it fantasy that we, too, were joined by a third presence? Did I tell you that wherever we walk, wherever the wayfarer, there is always this third presence ready to emerge from the shadows, and all in step along the dusty, stormy way."[1]

What a great testimony. Because of this day, our Lord will forever walk with you and me and all who claim the riches of the Christian life. What a day!

---

1. Malcolm Muggeridge, *Chronicles of Wasted Time* (Washington DC: Regnery Co., 1989), p. 162.

Easter 2
Acts 4:32-35

The Church's DNA

Once upon a time, a dear woman struggled to muster enough strength to face the trials that came her way. One worry after another seemed to pile up for her every day. Under the burden of it all, she became quite ill. Finally she went to see her doctor, a fine Christian gentleman who happened to know her and her family. He was aware of some of the disappointments and misfortunes the family had recently endured. He could find nothing organically wrong with the woman, but he told her that he was giving her a prescription that she must take every day for the rest of her life.

This was more than what she had imagined. What possibly could be wrong with her that she must be under prescriptive care every day for the rest of her life? The prospect of having huge drug bills and more doctor visits only added to her depression. The doctor suggested that she read over the prescription before she left the office, just to be sure she understood the dosage. She opened the slip of paper and this is what she read: "We know that in everything God works for good with those who love him."[1]

The early church communities certainly understood that the assurances of God's word are the best medicine that anyone can take. The awareness of God's merciful presence can heal our sin, lift our fallen spirits, and put vitality in living.

That was one of the essential elements of what it meant to be a church, the body of Christ. We are devoted to each other. We will care for each other and share good news at every level.

In our first lesson today, Luke gives us a glimpse of the DNA of the early church — characteristics and principles that have ensured strength of mission and purpose in every church since the first century.

He wants us to recognize how much their Easter faith had empowered their Spirit-filled and Spirit-led community. During those formative days, all had in common this profound conviction that the Lord was present among them. There was a deep awareness that God was at work among them.

The first principle was being a community of strong faith fully aware of the Lord's purpose for their lives and committed to support each other. One such example was their commitment to share every possession they had for the sake of the entire community. I don't think I have ever seen that, but I can imagine how strengthening that would be. The sensitivity to each other's needs, whether they are spiritual or physical, is critical to every church community.

The other compelling principle was the eagerness they all had to tell the Easter story, to build up the body of Christ, and to make disciples.

Fred Craddock tells the story about a parish he once served near Oak Ridge, Tennessee. Oak Ridge was booming at the time with the atomic energy initiative. The little town became a small city overnight. Every hill and every valley was teeming with motor homes, trucks, and temporary housing. People came from everywhere, many with their families. You can imagine how challenged the community was to accommodate these newcomers. Mr. Craddock indicated that their church was relatively close by. It was a beautiful little church. A white frame building that was 112 years old. The church had an organ in the corner, which a young boy had to pump while the organist played. The sanctuary was always beautifully decorated. Every pew was hand hewn from a giant poplar tree.

Pastor Craddock suggested one Sunday that they needed to launch an evangelism campaign in all the trailer parks and campgrounds to invite everybody to church. One of the council members responded, "Oh, I don't know. I don't think they would fit here." Another said, "It's just temporary, just construction people. They will be leaving soon."

"Well, we ought to invite them, make them feel at home," said Pastor Craddock.

They argued back and forth until a council member stood and said, "I move that in order to be a member of this church, you must own property in the county." "I second it," said another. The motion passed.

Several years later, Pastor Craddock took his wife back to their first parish community. It was different now. The parking lot was full. Motorcycles, trucks, and cars were parked in every space. And out front, there was a great big sign that read, "Barbecue, All You Can Eat!"

The Craddocks went inside. The pews were pushed against the wall. There were tables everywhere and tons of people, all kinds of people: Parthians, Medes, Edomites, and dwellers of Meso-potamia, all kinds of people.

Mr. Craddock leaned over to his wife and said, "It's a good thing this place is not a church, otherwise these people wouldn't be here."[2]

The early church was empowered and emboldened by the Easter faith. It was so energized that their mission was never in question. The core of its life was to proclaim the risen Lord, and this message was always accompanied with powerful signs and miracles. Unlike the little church in eastern Tennessee, the early church communities would have seized the moment, viewed their mission with clarity, and trusted the risen Christ to lead them to be faithful.

It is never easy, is it? In these days especially, we seem to have many more issues to grovel with. There is much more maintenance and programs to wrestle with. Our council agendas are filled with these necessities.

Occasionally someone says something or does something that reminds us of the early church and that simple but powerful Easter faith. Like the dear widow who took it upon herself to greet every new visitor after worship. She sat near the back so she could easily identify the newcomers. She was very cordial, very sincere. She loved the Lord and her church very much. That in itself always made an impression on the new folks. But what really caused them to reflect was her simple heartfelt witness. "If you decide to join our church, I promise you, you will never ever carry another burden alone."

That's a principle of the real church. It's in our DNA structure. May God continue to give us courage and conviction to be his people in our broken world.

---

1. Reuben K. Youngdahl, *Looking God's Way* (Minneapolis: Augsburg Publishing, 1966), p. 141.

2. Fred Craddock, *Craddock Stories* (St. Louis: Chalice Press, 2001), pp. 28-29.

Easter 3
Acts 3:12-19

At The Heart

We have a new library in town. I went over to check it out the other day by attending a bag lunch seminar.

As I walked in the front door, there was a huge sign that listed all the rooms and all the programs. Amazing. There were several seminars with guest lecturers listed. The seminar rooms were equipped with computers for PowerPoint presentations. Each had a small kitchen for refreshment preparation. Then there was a room full of computers. Each was occupied. A few people were standing in line waiting for an empty space. I also observed a research room. It contained a few tables and chairs, but most notably there was a large serving area with two receptionists and two computers nearby. "We can help you research most anything," said one.

I heard someone ask the other receptionist, "Where do they keep the books?"

Is it possible to have a library without books?

Our big megachurch in town lost its pastor last week. He is moving on to join the faculty of some church leadership school for pastors in Atlanta.

I remember the first time my wife and I visited this huge church facility in a gorgeous setting overlooking the mountains. Our friends had invited us to join them for lunch in the church cafeteria. It was on a Tuesday, as I recall. We had a delightful time. The meal was superb. There must have been a hundred people present enjoying a smorgasbord that would have put any restaurant to shame.

Someone asked if we would like a tour of the facilities. "Yes, of course," we said.

The dear lady took us on a 45-minute escapade. We visited the gymnasium, the fitness room, and the auditorium with screens, monitors, and twelve speakers. We saw the counseling center with a very cordial receptionist and four Christian counselors. We visited the media center and the family resource store. It was a magnificent ministry center.

Toward the end, I heard someone ask our guide, "Where is the sanctuary, the place where people worship and celebrate the eucharist?" I was embarrassed by the question, but I thought to myself, is it possible to have a church without a sanctuary, and worship, and faith? What is central to any church, anyway?

In our lesson for today, Peter is preaching from Solomon's portico. He chastises all the listeners for missing the point of God's gift of Jesus to them. He recites all the miscues including choosing the release of a criminal instead of Jesus at the big hearing before Pilate. "You really blew it!" says Peter. But God raised Jesus up from the dead anyway. We are witnesses to this fact!

Peter then turns to the crippled beggar he had just healed and speaks the truth to all his listeners. "And by faith in his name, his name itself has made this man strong, whom you see and know; and the faith that is through Jesus has given him this perfect health in the presence of all of you" (v. 16).

What is central to the church, any church?

What is most important to any life, a Christian life especially? Faith, faith, faith.

Peter is a perfect example as to the power of faith in human life.

The Bible tells us that faith can move mountains. Faith can generate enormous reserves of hope and love. It can transform any life to become more aware of God's presence and activity in the world.

How shall we define this critical component of life called faith? The writer of Hebrews defined it as ... "the assurance of things hoped for, the conviction of things not seen" (Hebrews 11:1).

John Calvin defined it as a confident knowledge of God's benevolence toward us, which is based on the gracious promise in Christ — revealed in our minds and confirmed in our hearts.

Howard Macy described faith as a response to God's initiative. God calls out first. God's yearning for us stirs up our longing in response. This response is faith.

Ken Gire describes faith as trust. Gire once prayed, "Dear God, someone once said that writing a novel is like driving at night with your headlights on — you can only see a few feet ahead, but you can make the entire trip that way. Living a life is like that, too, I think. Certainly a life of faith is. Give me the grace, O God, to live such a life ... and to realize that though the light given me is never as much as I would like, it is enough. It is enough."[1]

Faith is trusting God in all aspects of life.

Defined in these and similar ways, it is no exaggeration to conclude that without faith, whatever programs a church may have, it is not really a church. And might we also conclude that any life that is yearning and longing to rest secure in God's promises, regardless of the moments of struggle and doubt, understands just how precious God's gift of faith really is.

Faith becomes precious especially when we experience its strength during the tough times.

Years ago, Ernest Campbell, pastor of Riverside Church in New York, told of an interesting conversation he had with a college student at Lake Junaluska Conference Center in North Carolina. The young man was a PK (preacher's kid), very much loved and supported. He was contemplating the pastoral ministry but going through what he described as a mild crisis of faith. He confessed to this void in his life as, "I'm not sure what I believe."

Campbell, speaking out of love and genuine concern asked the young man a simple question: "What would you do with more faith now if you had it?" Campbell went on to suggest that the young man had few needs that really required faith:

- His parents were paying for his education.
- He had a nice support system at school.
- He had a loving home to go back to.
- All things were being provided for him.

"What do you need more faith for anyway?"[2]

It has been said in a variety of ways that God's gift of faith comes to those who really need it. Campbell went on to suggest that it is only as we attempt great things for God that we can expect great things from God. If we are content to play the *money game* or the *status game* or the *pleasure game*, we don't need faith for that! If we are 100% committed to our vocation in life, we don't need faith for that. But if we are trying to generate enough strength and courage to overcome some injustice or unbelief or loss of hope, God will give us faith. Lots of it.[3]

When life becomes challenging and difficult, that is when faith is precious.

In the final analysis, faith in Jesus Christ is a precious gift to the church and to individuals everywhere. May God continue to bless us with a deep awareness of his presence, power, and purpose.

---

1. Ken Gire, *Reflections on the Word* (Colorado Springs: Chariot Victor Publishing, 1998), p. 19.

2. *Twentieth Century Pulpit*, edited by James W. Cox (Abingdon, 1978), pp. 38-39.

3. *Ibid*, p. 39.

Easter 4
Acts 4:5-12

Confident Faith

It is hard to find a more bold expression of the Easter faith than what we hear from Peter today in our first lesson.

Peter and John had just healed a lame beggar at the gate of the temple. Without hesitation Peter proclaimed to the astonished crowd that the healing was the work of God who had raised Jesus from the dead. Almost immediately, the Sanhedrin arrests Peter and John and puts them on trial. They ask. "By what power or by what name did you do this?" (v. 7).

Filled with the Holy Spirit, reports Luke, Peter unleashes a profession of faith like no other. So bold and so confident Peter provides the context of the healing derived from the power of the risen Jesus from Nazareth, "The stone that was rejected by you, the builders" (v. 11). Nonetheless, God followed through anyway and accomplished his intentions. Peter uses this context to proclaim his Easter faith without flinching.

The story is an inspiration to all Christians especially to those who occasionally weaken and lose confidence and courage along their faith journey.

Some have suggested that doubt is the antithesis of faith. It may be logical, but in reality I think the antithesis is fear.

Once upon a time the devil held an auction of all his tools, jealousy, envy, hatred, revenge, greed, all of them. But the highest price tool of them all was fear. Someone asked the devil, "Why is fear priced the highest?" His answer was, "When everything else fails, this one always works."

Fear is the opposite of faith. Fear is what weakens us, makes us timid, bleeds our confidence, and dampens our enthusiasm about what God promises. The apostle Paul once said, "Do not worry about anything, but in everything by prayer and supplication with thanksgiving let your requests be made known to God. And the peace of God, which surpasses all understanding, will guard your hearts and your minds in Christ Jesus" (Philippians 4:5-7). Paul also reminded us, "I can do all things through him who strengthens me" (Philippians 4:13).

Fear breaks our spirits. Faith reminds us that God can be trusted. "Even though I walk through the darkest valley, I fear no evil; for you are with me" (Psalm 23:4).

No psalm exudes the spirit of confident faith better than the Psalm 23. "The Lord is my shepherd, I shall not want" (Psalm 23:1). Few biblical metaphors and images depict this special relationship we can enjoy with our Lord more dramatically than the concept of the *good shepherd*. Most of us have never seen a shepherd, but we get the picture anyway. The imagery is filled with compassion, mercy, faithfulness, commitment, kindness and the ever-present care of our Father God. "The Lord is my shepherd ... I will fear no evil." We are God's children. We have hope and faith as gifts of God. We have the promise now and in the life to come.

Once upon a time, a pastor was sitting at the bedside of a 93-year-old member of his flock. The dear lady was conscious but clinging to life. As the pastor prayed with the lady while holding her hand, he suddenly began to recite Psalm 23. Toward the conclusion, the dear lady smiled with eyes closed and joined her pastor, "Surely goodness and mercy shall follow me all the days of my life; and I shall dwell in the house of the good Lord," she interjected, "forever."

Confident faith? You bet! She was at peace, unafraid, trusting in the good Lord's promises.

On the other hand, fear and anxiety occasionally creep into our lives like a cloud. They overshadow everything. They can make us physically and emotionally sick. They can even erode our faith.

The escape of fear's dreadful claim on us doesn't have to be terribly difficult. The first step in seeking release can simply be to take the hand of God extended to us in any dark hour.

Bill Hinson, a Methodist pastor, once told a story about growing up on a farm in Georgia. He had one chore that terrified him.

During the fall when his father had to mind the furnace in the tobacco barn late every evening, Bill had the responsibility to take his father's dinner to him. The barn seemed a mile away, though in reality it was only a few hundred yards from their home. Invariably, it was dark when the young boy had to make his trip.

Pastor Hinson still remembers how frightened he was by all the sounds and shadows. Wind would rustle the fallen leaves. Images of scary things lurked from every direction. Pastor Hinson reported walking down the very middle of the country road avoiding all the monsters on each side. By the time he reached the barn he was literally trembling with fear and could hardly breathe. He would then have to turn around and walk all the way back home through the dark. One time there was a special evening he never forgot. He was too proud to tell his dad how frightened he was, but somehow his dad became aware of it. After he finished his dinner, his dad said, "I think I need to report something to your mom. Maybe I'll just walk back home with you this evening."

With that, the father extended his hand and the boy reached up to take it. On the trip home, Hinson exclaimed, "Every frightening thing stayed in its place!"[1]

Confident faith is a precious gift, isn't it? As the gift is offered and we accept it in trust, life is never sweeter.

---

1. William H. Hinson, *Reshaping the Inner You* (San Francisco: Harper & Row Publishing, 1988), p. 69.

Easter 5
Acts 8:26-40

A Wonderful Conversion Story

In our first lesson today, we hear yet another Easter faith story. It's the story of the conversion of the Ethiopian eunuch, a God-fearing minister of Queen Candace. The eunuch had just been to Jerusalem to worship. Now he was returning home. As he sat in his chariot reading the prophet Isaiah, Philip introduces himself and upon invitation begins to interpret the Isaiah text. It turned out to be a witnessing opportunity to the good news about Jesus. The eunuch responds to Philip's teaching and also to the prompting of the Holy Spirit. Eventually, a baptism occurs that solidifies the faith of yet another convert.

It's a beautiful story.

The first thing that is so impressive about the story is the eagerness of the Ethiopian eunuch to learn about God, to discern what God's plans might be for him to grow in faith and truth. He was very eager to have Philip explain the scriptures so he could better understand the truth and will of God.

Sometimes our lives become so helter-skelter that we become disoriented in our faith journey. So many things compete for our time and priority. Sometimes we end up devoting most of our time to entities that are counterfeit and unimportant.

Once upon a time, Fred Craddock, a popular preacher and storyteller, told of an incident he swears to be true.

Dr. Craddock was visiting in the home of one of his former students. After dinner, the young couple cleared the table and went to the kitchen, leaving Fred in the living room to visit with the family dog, a sleek greyhound. While getting acquainted with the dog, the dog turned to Fred and asked, "Is this your first visit to Connecticut?"

"No," answered Dr. Craddock, "I attended school in New England years ago."

"Well," responded the greyhound, "I guess you heard I came up here from Miami?"

"I did," said Dr. Craddock. "You are retired, aren't you?"

"No, no," said the greyhound. "I didn't retire. I must tell you, I spent ten years as a professional racing greyhound. That, of course, means ten years of running around a track day after day, seven days a week with friends and relatives, chasing a rabbit. You know what I'm referring to. Well, one day, I got up really close to that rabbit to discover it was a fake! Can you believe it? I had spent my whole professional life chasing a fake rabbit! Let me tell you, I didn't retire. I quit."[1]

The Ethiopian eunuch appeared to have a passion for the scriptures and an eagerness to keep his faith walk a priority. Luke goes into great detail to explain the circumstances that led up to his conversion.

His relationship and his understanding of the Lord were top priorities.

As we hear the story and reflect about our own faith journey, we recognize there may be times when we chase the fake rabbits instead of devoting more time and energy to *the truth and the life* that is in Jesus Christ.

Dag Hammarskjold said it so beautifully in his work titled, *Markings*. "The best and most wonderful thing that can happen to you in this life, is that you should sit silently and let God work and speak."[2]

Our eagerness to pursue many things in life can often lead us down empty paths. Many of the perceived rainbows end up being fruitless. We wind up exhausted and disoriented. But it doesn't have to be that way.

The second notable aspect of our story is the Ethiopian eunuch's openness to the Holy Spirit. Luke refers to the prompting and work of the Holy Spirit over and over again. He wants his listeners to recognize how important God's activity through the Holy Spirit really is. Through the faithful witness of Philip, the Ethiopian eunuch was converted to Christianity by the Holy Spirit.

We have God's gifts, too, in our own baptism. The Holy Spirit will always be a conduit to a life of faith, purpose, and fulfillment. Sometimes, however, the energy is not as strong and recognizable as we would like.

Once upon a time, a missionary in Kenya was given a car to help him in his missionary rounds, going from village to village to preach and teach the Bible and so forth. After he had the car a few months, it refused to start. He looked under the hood, but not knowing anything about engines, he presumed the battery was worn out. He found, however, that he could get his started by getting some boys from a local school to push the car fifty feet or so, or he could park it headed down hill, and roll it off, engaging the clutch. For two years, he endured this routine. Then the time came to talk his family back to the United States. Before he left Africa, his replacement arrived. The old missionary showed his replacement his car, and described the ways to push it or roll it off to get it started. The new missionary looked under the hood for a moment, then said, "Doctor, I think that the battery cable has come loose from the starter." The new missionary reconnected the loose cable, got in the driver's seat, turned the key, pressed the starter, and the engine roared to life.[3]

Our story today reminds us how faithful God is in providing us with the resources we need for faithful living. It is all a gift. May God continue to work at keeping us connected to his love and mercy in Jesus Christ. May we be sensitive to the Holy Spirit among us to provide the energy, courage, and strength to be God's people.

---

1. www.day1.net/index.php5?view=transcripts&tid=507.

2. Dag Hammarskjold, *Markings* (New York: Alfred A. Knopf, 1964), p. 106.

3. www.st-matthew.org/audio/co2007056.pdf.

Easter 6
Acts 10:44-48

Our Salvation In Being Loved

All of a sudden, the Holy Spirit fell on everyone, even the Gentiles. No one was more surprised than Peter and the Jewish converts. Up to this point, they thought the risen Christ was a gift just to them. But now, with the baptism of Cornelius and this massive gift of the Holy Spirit, everything is turned upside down. What a surprise. And yet, when we think about it, that is not the first time God surprises his people. Scripture is filled with stories and examples.

The stories sometimes seem conflicting and contradictory. The biggest example was when Jesus died. New life was given to generations of people. Dying became rising. Death became life.

Jesus' ministry itself was often confusing. Prostitutes became heroes of the faith. Foreigners became even more saintly than did the religious elite. The poor and the outcast had a more distinctive advantage of membership in the new kingdom than did the scholarly and the faithful. At the time of Jesus' birth, God was initiating the unexpected as well. They had been waiting two or three centuries for the Messiah's coming. They were looking everywhere for him, and every time they saw someone eclectic and charismatic, like John the Baptist, they pondered whether he might be the one. The hope of his coming literally kept them alive through the exile and through oppressive times with Rome.

When he did come, they didn't recognize him. They did not recognize him because he came quietly instead of in a fanfare. They expected a Messiah that would liberate them from Rome. He didn't. He liberated them from sin, fear, and guilt. They expected a Christ who would perform all kinds of majestic feats, like jumping off the temple. He didn't. He fed the poor. He sat with children. He healed the broken. He stood by the lonely.

In the end they expected their Messiah to be a smashing success whereas, in *their* reality, he was a dismal failure.

It seems God never ceases to surprise us, turning things upside down, blessing us when we least expect it.

Several years ago, Theodore Parker Ferris told a radio audience in Boston, Massachusetts, how some of life's events and experiences remind us that life can be lost before it is ever really lived.

There are all kinds of examples: the sudden death of a child, years of unhappiness or illness that depletes most of life's energy, living in a home that has no love either to give or to receive. Sometimes a life can be so paralyzed by fear and disappointment that it never has a chance to break out and enjoy the best.

Listen to what one man wrote when he was only 32 years old. "I am now the most miserable man living. If what I feel were equally distributed to the whole human family, there would not be one cheerful face on earth. Whether I shall ever be better I cannot tell."

Abraham Lincoln wrote those words. It doesn't sound like him, does it? The words remind us of another more important truth and that is, the Christian life, the life of faith, hope, and promise can be saved long after it seems to have been lost.[1]

Our story today, when God sent forth his Holy Spirit to all gathered, Jews and Gentiles alike, reminds us how generous and loving God really is. God's strongest desire is to save us, bless us, and restore life to the fullest.

Woodrow Wilson had a very difficult life in many respects, especially early on.

In the second term of his law school training in Virginia he had a nervous breakdown and during that period he wrote, "How can a man with a weak body ever arrive anywhere?" Later he married a wonderful woman and this is what he wrote to her: "You are the only person in the world with whom I do not have to act a part. To whom I do not have to deal out confidences cautiously ... My salvation is in being loved."[2]

You and I know of another love just like that and even more so. It is the unconditional, permanent love of Christ. It is a gift for the taking, a reality that only requires trust and an open heart.

One of the great spiritual writers of our time is Father Henri Nouwen, a priest devoted to helping Christians throughout the world understand how committed God is to save us and love us through our Lord Jesus Christ.

In his little book, *With Open Hands*, he writes about how difficult it is for some people at different times to accept the free gifts of God and give up those things that constrict our hearts and minds. In the book, Nouwen tells the story about an elderly woman brought to a psychiatric hospital as an example of this resistant behavior.

> *She was wild, swinging at everything in sight, and frightening everyone so much so that the doctors had to take everything away from her. But there was one small coin which she gripped in her fist and would not give up. In fact, it took two people to pry open that clenched hand. It was as though she would lose her very self along with the coin if she let go. If they deprived her of that last possession, she would have nothing more and be nothing more. That was her fear.*
>
> *When you are invited to pray, you are asked to open your tightly clenched fist and give up your last coin....*
>
> *To pray means to open your hands before God. It means slowly relaxing the tension which squeezes your hands together and accepting your existence with an increasing readiness, not as a possession to defend, but as a gift to receive.*[3]

Opening our hands before God, relaxing the tension, accepting our existence as a gift — what a great way to live.

Let us pray with Father Nouwen.

> *Dear God,*
> *I am so afraid to open my clenched fists!*
> *Who will I be when I have nothing left to hold on to?*
> *Who will I be when I stand before you with my empty hands?*
> *Please help me to gradually open my hands*
> *and to discover that I am not what I own,*
> *but what you want to give me.*

*And what you want to give me is love,
unconditional, everlasting love. Amen.*[4]

---

1. T. P. Ferris, *This is the Day* (Dublin, New Hampshire: Yankee Publishing, 1976), pp. 231-232.

2. *Ibid*, p. 235.

3. Henri Nouwen, *With Open Hands* (Notre Dame, Indiana: Ave Maria Press, 1995), pp. 61-62.

4. *Ibid*.

The Ascension Of Our Lord
Acts 1:1-11

Life's Greatest Tension: Despair vs. Hope

Today is Ascension Sunday.

Today we commemorate the day when Jesus bid farewell to his followers and friends and ascended into heaven to sit at the right hand of the Father.

In some ways it's an anxious day. "How will we go on without him?" they surely whispered among themselves. "How can we possibly maintain the strength and perspective — the motivation to live according to his teachings and promises? How can we live with determination and purpose if he is not here to sustain us?"

We, too, have that concern from time to time when we sense an absence and share the notion that maybe the good Lord has left us to be alone with the demons of the world. We have that concern in times when the newspapers confound us and the events all around us seem to suggest that God isn't paying attention.

Fear and anxiety are realities in every age, but for the followers of Jesus so is the power and presence of the risen Lord, ascended into heaven.

The disciples would soon experience this positive reality as they separated and began to preach, teach, and heal throughout the existing world. The power of the risen Lord — ascended into heaven would soon transform the world through them as they faithfully served in his holy name.

The apostle Paul was one of those stalwarts of the faith. His letter to the Ephesians was written to this new community in Christ. He was eager to be faithful but occasionally was also susceptible to the fear and anxiety that perplexes every Christian generation.

Paul encourages the church at Ephesus so beautifully. "I pray that the God of our Lord Jesus ... may give you a spirit of wisdom and revelation as you come to know him, so that with eyes of your heart enlightened you may know the hope ... riches ... the immeasurable greatness of his power" (Ephesians 1:17-19).

We gather again to be renewed and strengthened by this wonderful good news.

We gather amidst enormous tragedy in our world, our communities, and perhaps even in our very personal lives to hear a word of hope and truth. Christ is alive in power. He is fully present. He is fully active in bringing about his purposes in spite of what occasionally appears to be just the opposite.

Many years ago under the leadership of benevolent kings and queens, architects and builders were brought from Constantinople to an area east of the Black Sea to build huge churches out of local rock. Their Byzantine churches were monuments, full of exquisite arches, frescoes, and stonework, many of which survive today, but only as ruins. The age of Christianity is over in that part of the world. The Mongols conquered the area in the thirteenth century. Civilization moved west and east. The last baptisms took place in the 1800s. Now the area is predominantly Muslim, as is the rest of Turkey. Meanwhile, the descendants of those ancient builders have become farmers, who still pluck old roof tiles and gargoyle parts out of their fields as they plow in the spring.

If you go there today, you can find the remains of the great churches deep in the countryside with what is left of their high walls poking up through the canopy of trees. All of the good carvings have been carried away, along with many of the building stones, which local people have quarried for their own houses.

The churches are multipurpose buildings now, serving as soccer fields, sheep pens, and garbage dumps. The roofs are gone. So are the doors, floors, and altars. All that is left are the walls, a few broken columns, and here and there the traces of an old fresco that has somehow survived the years. Occasionally, you might see a part of a fresco with a faded scarred image of Christ with three fingers raised in a familiar fashion.

In a strange way, the Lord is still giving his blessing to a ruined church.[1]

We are not a ruined church by any means, even though we know of some congregations who have somehow lost traction and perhaps courage.

The point is the Lord Christ continues to give his blessing no matter what, in spite of us at times. His blessing will prevail, sooner or later. God is at work all around us. We are his chosen instruments of reconciliation in the world. Paul says the church shall be a community of heaven on earth.

From the heart of Christ's body shall flow all the transforming love of God, bestowing hope, bestowing courage and immeasurable power and greatness.

What does all that have to say to you and me in the great scheme of things?

May I suggest just this one thing? Because God is at work in Jesus Christ all around us, we will choose not to be fearful, negative, or hopeless. Instead, we will choose to be observant and alert to God's activity, his love and power, and his determination to bless and redeem all of us. We will choose to be confident in the Lord and constantly be on the look out for his work among us. All the while, the apostles and all the saints pray for us that the eyes of our hearts will be opened so that we can see the great power of God at work all around us.

Barbara Brown Taylor tells a touching story of this reality in her book, *Home By Another Way*.

There was a woman with recurrent cancer who was told she had six months to live. Her church gathered around her and her husband, extending help in all sorts of ways. It was even suggested by one to give the woman a foot massage and paint her toenails. That lifted her spirits, as you can imagine. She prepared for death but to her surprise, she got better.

On Christmas Eve, she was back in church for the first time in months with an oxygen tank in tow. After the first hymn, she made her way to the lectern to read the lesson from Isaiah. The sounds of her oxygen tank and her laboring voice were noticeable. Every candle in the sanctuary glittered in her eyes. "Strengthen the weak hands, and make firm the feeble knees. Say to those who are of a fearful heart, 'Be strong, do not fear! Here is your God' " (Isaiah 35:3-4). When she sat down, the congregation knew they had not just heard the word of the Lord. They had seen it in action as well.[2]

Christ is alive in power. We will not fear because we know it is so very true.

---

1. www.preaching.org/classroom/display_article/16.

2. Barbara Brown Taylor, *Home By Another Way* (Cambridge, Massachusetts: Cowley Publications, 1999), p. 201.

Easter 7
Acts 1:15-17, 21-26

The Courage To Carry On

The courage to be, to do, to act, to care, and to be responsible lies at the heart of our existence. It is a challenge that occurs more than once during a lifetime. There are moments when we are tempted to give up and say, "What's the use?" Yet, there is usually something within us that encourages us — leads us, in fact — to carry on.

The apostles were at such a crossroads in our first lesson for today. We celebrate the Sunday after the Ascension Of Our Lord or the Seventh Sunday Of Easter. The apostles were living in the "in between" times. Most were probably still grieving, struggling to carry on after their tremendous loss. One could imagine how easy it would have been for any one of them to say, "I can't go on. I'm tired of being on an emotional string. I've had enough. I'm going back to a life that is safe and predictable." We can understand how that reaction would have been possible.

We also understand how life, for the most part, is not lived by clear-cut choices and objectives, as we might prefer, but by circumstances and courageous, unclear choices. John Lennon once said something to the effect that, life is what happens to us while we are making other plans.

Christians tend to see it a little differently. We usually understand our journey in context with grace and faith; in terms of a blessing at Baptism that initiates a guiding influence and a presence. We eventually come to an understanding of our life's journey in terms of being chosen by God and empowered by God's love to carry on, of living expectantly and anticipating God's activity at most any juncture.

Our disciples certainly understood these principles of faith, courage, and purpose. In our lesson, Luke explains how the twelve (eleven, as it were) served as a vital link between the ascended Christ and the church. Amidst their grief they continued to carry on. Scripture was fulfilled with respect to the fate of Judas. Secondly, the twelve were reconstituted with the choice of his successor.

I think there are two very important lessons for us in our story today. First of all, the courage to carry on is often a gift of faith and usually is in context with a mission and purpose in life.

I'm familiar with the layers of discouragement that can happen to us and the bombardment of unfortunate events that can sap our energy and deplete every ounce of motivation. We've been there, done that. But I'm not talking about the sad times. I'm talking about purpose in life, our choices, our perspective, and our opportunities. It's a much bigger picture.

Perhaps to understand it most clearly is to understand the fact that God gives each one of us some opportunity to give and work toward something that matters greatly. The apostles understood what was on the line. They understood the opportunity and the mission.

In our experiences of courage to carry on, we must relearn the truth: Genuine motivation in life comes from choosing to give. That's tough for a culture that has learned how to be on the receiving end very comfortably most of time. But *receiving* never satisfies like *giving*.

Best-selling author and sports writer, Mitch Albom, in a recent article in Northwest Airline's *World Traveler* magazine described the unique relationship he had with Morrie Schwartz, a former professor. One time, Albom confronted Professor Schwartz for always helping others with their problems. "You have bigger problems than they do," said Albom. To which Morrie replied, "Why would I take from people ... taking makes me feel like I'm dying. Giving makes me feel like I'm living."

"That sentence has never left me," said Albom.[1]

Courage, being truly alive and being enthused with life is always connected in some way to giving ... always!

Will Willimon once related to a group of Duke students at worship that Christian discipleship is never trivial, unimportant, or easy. Willimon said it is, in fact, always energy producing. He then went on to tell a story about a recruiter from Teach America who addressed a crowd at Duke a few years ago. In case you are unfamiliar with Teach America, it is an organization that recruits the nation's best college and university students to go and teach in the most impossible teaching situations in the nation.[2]

This recruiter from Teach America scanned the crowd of Duke students. She began by saying: "I don't really know why I am here tonight. I can tell just by looking at you that you are probably uninterested in what I have to say. This is one of the best universities in America. You are all successful. That is why you are here, to become an even greater success on Madison Avenue or Wall Street or in law school. And here I stand, trying to recruit some people for the most difficult job you will ever have in your life. I'm out looking for people who want to go into a burned-out classroom in Watts and teach biology. I'm looking for somebody to go into a little one-room schoolhouse in West Virginia and teach kids from six years to thirteen yours old how to read. We had three teachers killed last year in their classrooms! And I can tell, just by looking at you, that none of you want to throw away your lives on anything like that. One the other hand, if by chance there is somebody here who may be interested, I've got these brochures and I am going to leave them down here and will be glad to speak to anybody who is interested. The meeting is over."[3]

Willimon said all the students jumped up, rushed to the aisles, and ran down to the front, scrambling for pamphlets and applications to Teach America.

Would you agree that most people are eager to give their lives to something more important than themselves? Can you get a glimpse of why the apostles were so committed and encouraged to get on with their mission?

Where might you be along your life's journey? Do you look forward to each day? Are you engaged in something that requires you to give, not take all the time? Is there a zest for life and a perspective of purpose and partnership with God to share with you?

The second lesson of the text is very simple but extremely important. When the apostles chose a process to determine Judas' replacement, they decided to cast lots.

When you call a pastor would you consider lining up a few candidates and drawing straws? You probably would not. We have a much more sophisticated process these days. But think about it as a matter of trusting God to choose and reveal. Is that stupid or is it an expression of confidence, faith, and complete trust in God?

We can learn from the story. Intimate relationships with Christ leads to confidence, strong faith, and yes, complete trust that everything is in the Lord's good keeping.

That's a good way to live, is it not? It's probably the only way to live as Christian disciples.

---

1. Jane Ammeson, "Do the Right Thing," *NWA World Traveler*, August/September 2007, p. 52.

2. www.chapel.duke.edu/worship/Sunday/viewsermon.aspx?id=11, p. 4.

3. *Ibid*, pp. 4-5.

www.ingramcontent.com/pod-product-compliance
Lightning Source LLC
Chambersburg PA
CBHW071411040426
42444CB00009B/2202